Why Would Anyone Get Married?

DAVID J. AYERS

C·C

Why Would Anyone Get Married?
By David J. Ayers

© 2022 Core Christianity
13230 Evening Creek Drive
Suite 220-222
San Diego, CA 92128

Design and Creative Direction by Metaleap Creative

Printed in the United States of America

First Printing—February 2022

CONTENTS

Do You Know the Basic Realities of Marriage?

When my wife and I got married in 1982, I'd been a Christian for about five years. I'd been "saved" out of what we called at the time "freak" culture through the 1970's-era Jesus Movement. She'd grown up in a rural, conservative Methodist church. Neither of us had ever been exposed to any systematic, doctrinally grounded teaching on Christian marriage.

We both wanted a godly marriage. But beyond a few basics—don't commit adultery, try not to get divorced, pray and study the Bible together, be kind to each other, don't go to sleep angry, and so on—we didn't understand God's parameters and purposes for marriage.

This was true even for things as elemental as "don't have sex until you're married." Don't get me wrong—we knew that fornication was a sin. We knew the relevant Bible rules and that they protected us from undesirable consequences such as out-of-wedlock pregnancy and sexually transmitted infections. But we didn't know the deeper theological meaning of the relationship between sex and marriage. There were other gaps in our understanding of Christian marriage as well.

We're much better grounded now in a biblical theology of marriage, and our marital union and our children are better off as a result. However, it would have been wonderful if we'd we learned those things much earlier, ideally before we got married. It makes me sad, as a long-term Christian college professor, to see that now—forty years later—most

3

of my students are no better educated on this issue than I was at their age. Many will carry this ignorance into their marriages.

We believers who are called to be married ought to desire "good marriages." Who wouldn't? But for Christians, a "good marriage" is one that fulfills the wise purposes of our sovereign Lord. We're called to conform our individual marriages to the general ends for which God created marriage—defining it as he defines it and living out the implications of his definition. It means finding our liberty, happiness, and contentment within the order he has established and not forming marital unions to suit our fashions and desires.

We know that God created marriage at the beginning. It's the first social institution—the first ordered set of roles, obligations, rights, and shared purposes uniting people. The welfare of the entire social order ultimately rested upon its shoulders. In its absence or brokenness no healthy society could ever exist. He made the first man and first woman, united in wedlock by God himself, partners in ruling the earth—co-regents of the planet (Gen. 1:26–30, 2:18, 20b–24).

He also invested marriage with spiritual realities that are powerful, mysterious, and wonderful in so many ways and yet not fully comprehensible to us. He designed marriage to represent—even embody—the mystical union of Christ and his people (Eph. 5:22–32). In a fallen world, a godly Christian marriage is a powerful gospel witness. In the godly husband there's Christ, sacrificing himself for his people, loving, protecting, and nurturing them (Eph. 5:25–30). In the godly wife, there's the church, honoring, serving, submitting to (Eph. 5:22–24), and loving the one who has set his love on her.

What a powerful picture! What a wonderful calling that every Christian marriage has.

In this booklet, I briefly set forth God's design for marriage, the implications of this for our marriages, and some key practical ways we can nurture the elements of this design. By "design" I mean two things. First, what marriage *is*, in essence—God's basic definition by which we know the real thing when we see it and live it, and by which we identify counterfeits or serious error. Second, what marriage is *for*. Its purposes, its end.

The chapters are organized that way. In the first, we lay out God's definition of marriage and consider some of its implications. Each of the next three chapters tackle one of the three major purposes for marriage that the Bible and most of the historic church has recognized: a legitimate and holy sexual relationship, mutual help and companionship, and the procreation of children.

There are numerous confessions and statements that describe these basic realities of Christian marriage. Let me finish this introduction with my personal favorite, one that's theologically accurate, succinct, and beautifully worded. I can't think of a better way to frame the incredible wisdom and stunning beauty of the institution called "marriage" that I want to explore with you here. It comes from the "Form for the Solemnization of Matrimony" in the 1662 Church of England Book of Common Prayer.

Dearly beloved, we are gathered together here in the sight of God, and in the face of this Congregation, to join together this man and this woman in holy Matrimony; which is an honourable estate, instituted of God in the time of man's innocency, signifying unto us the mystical union that is betwixt Christ and his Church; which holy estate Christ adorned and beautified with his presence, and first miracle that he wrought, in Cana of Galilee; and is commended of Saint Paul to be honourable among all men: and therefore is not by any to be enterprised, nor taken in hand, unadvisedly, lightly, or wantonly, to satisfy men's carnal lusts and appetites, like brute beasts that have no understanding; but reverently, discreetly, advisedly, soberly, and in the fear of God; duly considering the causes for which Matrimony was ordained.

First, It was ordained for the procreation of children, to be brought up in the fear and nurture of the Lord, and to the praise of his holy Name.

Secondly, It was ordained for a remedy against sin, and to avoid fornication; that such persons as have not the gift of continency might marry, and keep themselves undefiled members of Christ's body.

Thirdly, It was ordained for the mutual society, help, and comfort, that the one ought to have of the other, both in prosperity and adversity. Into which holy estate these two persons present come now to be joined. Therefore if any man can shew any just cause, why they may not lawfully be joined together, let him now speak, or else hereafter for ever hold his peace.[1]

---

1   The Book of Common Prayer, introduction by James Wood (New York: Penguin Books, 2012), 311.

WHY WOULD ANYONE GET MARRIED?

CHAPTER ONE

What Is Marriage?

To live out something well, you must understand it. To understand something, you must have a good definition. That makes sense, right? If I don't know what something is beyond a vague notion, how do I know the real thing when I see it? How can I distinguish the genuine from the counterfeit? How do I know I'm doing something well if I don't really know what it is? Ignoring the need for good definitions is a common mistake. People often try to persuade others of things they can't clearly define.

This is certainly true about marriage, especially given how contested it's become culturally. Our understanding of marriage is increasingly a product of *expressive individualism*. In the 1980s, a team of sociologists led by Robert Bellah showed how this had come to characterize how most Americans viewed marriage. Here's how they defined it: "Expressive individualism holds that each person has a unique core of feeling and intuition that should unfold or be expressed if individuality is to be realized." They connected this to modern psychotherapy, which emphasizes strong emotions and self-discovery.[1]

Marriage is now seen mainly as a vehicle for meeting individual needs and desires. It's a means to self-fulfillment. Sociologist Andrew Cherlin described this modern outlook on marriage: "Each person should develop a fulfilling, independent self instead of merely sacrificing oneself to one's

---

1 Robert Bellah, et al. *Habits of the Heart: Individualism and Commitment in American Life* (New York: Harper & Row, 1985), 333–334. For a powerful and up-to-date intellectual and social history of expressive individualism, see Carl Trueman's *The Rise and Triumph of the Modern Self: Cultural Amnesia, Expressive Individualism, and the Road to the Sexual Revolution* (Wheaton: Crossway, 2020).

partner."[2] In his college text, he adds this: "Feeling that you [are] meeting your obligations to others [is] less central; feeling that you [have] opportunities to grow as a person [is] more central."[3] With this, he notes, marital options are increasingly selected from a growing palette of choices, including the choice to not marry at all, or to live together even while unmarried, having sex, or having children.[4]

Considering this, it's not surprising that same-sex marriage is now legal and accepted by the majority of Americans. This and other distortions of marriage naturally flow from this idea that we mainly define marriage around our shifting, man-centered ideas and aspirations. We expect that law will eventually follow, if and when our preferred perspectives and practices become broadly accepted.

This entire approach is alien to God's definition of marriage as taught in the Bible. Biblical marriage certainly provides for human happiness and flourishing in many ways. It ought to include at the center a loving, mutually satisfying relationship. But it does so in ways that are almost opposite to expressive individualism. God calls married people to mutual giving and sacrifice, to embrace an order with boundaries and rules established when God created humanity, to exercise self-control and humility, to have a permanent commitment sealed by a solemn covenant, and so on. God's way involves accepting his role as the Creator and Sovereign Lord of marriage and submitting to his design for it. It's what God says marriage is that counts, not how we mortals choose to create or define it for ourselves.

Yet the expressive individualist understanding of marriage is increasingly

---

2 Andrew Cherlin, "The Deinstitutionalization of Marriage," *Journal of Marriage and Family* 66. No. 4 (November 2004): 848–861, 852.

3 Andrew Cherlin, *Public and Private Families: An Introduction.* 8th ed. (New York: McGraw-Hill, 2016), 194.

4 Cherlin, "The Deinstitutionalization of Marriage," 853.

embraced by professing evangelicals.[5] With each successive generation, we're drifting further from God's design. It's time to reacquaint ourselves with God's definition of marriage and consider its implications for our own marriages. Here are seven truths that make up the definition of marriage:[6]

1. MARRIAGE IS CREATED BY GOD, WITH A DEFINITE SHAPE.

The first reality we must acknowledge is that marriage is created by God. It was his design. It didn't evolve from primitive societies with no marital bonds but is essential and basic to human social life. Marriage isn't a social construct or human invention. This is shown in Genesis 1:27–28 and, especially, 2:18–24.

Like everything God created, marriage has a definite shape. Across cultures or even among individual couples within a culture, there's legitimate variation in how people practice and experience it. But if certain essential things aren't there, no human relationship is a true marriage, no matter what people call it.

---

5   As I and others have documented, this is clear in our ideas and practices about sex outside marriage, divorce, cohabitation, and even same-sex marriage, as well as matrimony itself. See the following which I have authored: *Christian Marriage: A Comprehensive Introduction* (Bellingham: Lexham Press, 2019), especially the chapters on sex outside marriage and divorce; *After the Revolution: Sex and the Single Evangelical* (Bellingham: Lexham Press, 2022); "First Comes Love, Then Comes House Keys," *Christianity Today*, April 2021, 36-41; "Unhappily Married or Happily Divorced? The False Dilemma," *Modern Reformation*, January 25, 2021, https://modernreformation.org/resource-library/web-exclusive-articles/the-mod-unhappily-married-or-happily-divorced-the-false-dilemma/; "Young American Catholics and the Normalization of Lesbian and Gay Sexuality," *Crisis Magazine*, May 19, 2021, https://www.crisismagazine.com/2021/young-american-catholics-and-the-normalization-of-lesbian-and-gay-sexuality. (The latter was written for a Catholic magazine but compares them with and documents Evangelical Protestant realities.)

6   I can't deal with every aspect of the definition of marriage here. See Chapter One of *Christian Marriage* for a more detailed treatment.

2. MARRIAGE IS A SEXUAL UNION.

By "sexual" I mean procreative in nature, whether or not a particular couple is ultimately able to bear children. Certainly, having sex doesn't in itself make a couple married. If that were true, then the Samaritan woman would have been married rather than, as Jesus said to her, having been married numerous times but now with a man who was not her husband (John 4:17–18).[7] We can add that if tragic events, the decline of age, infirmity, or imprisonment cause a couple to be separated sexually at some point, a couple who was lawfully married remains united in wedlock.

However, without sexual intercourse, there's no true marriage. This is why in many places, including English Common Law and even in many American states, a licensed marriage can be "annulled" for something called "failure to consummate." An annulment is a declaration that no true marriage ever took place. It's not the same thing as divorce, which ends a real marriage.

This idea that couples must have united sexually to be married is entirely biblical. The procreative act was built into marriage from the beginning (see for example Gen. 1:28; 4:1). In fact, the proof of virginity required by Old Testament law shows that Hebrew couples were expected to have sex following their wedding ceremony (Deut. 22:13–21).[8] God created sex to be delightful and gave most of us a natural desire for it. He blesses us in doing what he wants married couples to do. In fact, we find the apostle Paul warning married people against neglecting their sexual relationships (1 Cor. 7:5).[9]

---

7 *Christian Marriage*, 26.

8 *Christian Marriage*, 25.

9 We'll get into the sexual relationship in greater detail in the next chapter.

3. MARRIAGE IS BY DEFINITION HETEROSEXUAL.

This is obvious from our last point. Marriage unites a man and a woman. This is clear from the very beginning, as we see in the foundational Genesis passages. Same-sex marriage may be legal in the United States and many other countries, but it's a legal fiction. As my mother used to say, "Calling it something doesn't make it so."

Marriage is the union of a man and a woman not simply because marital sex and procreation requires it. In marriage, man and woman are complementary aspects of a larger whole.[10] They're different in ways that fit each other. This radiates through all aspects of the marital relationship and is something to celebrate (see Eph. 5:22–33).

4. MARRIAGE IS MONOGAMOUS.

God wants us to be married to only one partner at a time. He gave Adam only one woman to be his wife. This can be confusing to Christians because in much of the Old Testament period God allowed men to have more than one wife, though the practice was strictly regulated, mostly to protect women (Exod. 21:10–11; Deut. 12:15–17; Lev. 18:18). Like some of the divorce laws, this seems to have partly been a concession to their "hardness of heart" (see, for example, Mark 10:5 and Matt. 19:8).

However, Jesus made strong statements forbidding spouses from marrying another person as long as the first spouse is alive, except for grave reasons justifying divorce (Mark 10:11–12, Matt. 19:9). He also explicitly rooted his marriage teaching in creation, pointing to Adam and Eve's monogamous relationship (see, for example, Matt. 19:4–6 and

---

10 We'll explore the "larger whole" aspect more below.

Mark 10:6–9). Christians have recognized from the earliest days of the church that monogamy is God's intention for marriage.[11] All major wings of orthodox Christianity embrace this truth.

Most of us aren't going to practice polygamy. But we know that God's commandments apply not only to our external action but also to our minds and hearts (see for example Matt. 5:22, 28). This includes honoring our marriages in our thoughts and desires. I'm not just speaking here about not committing adultery with our bodies, minds, eyes, or hearts (Matt. 22:27–30), as important as that is. Embracing monogamy also means never wishing you were married to anyone else or had married someone different than your spouse. No daydreaming about what could have been. Our spouses are to have an exclusive, exalted position in our lives, which we guard carefully in all respects.

5. MARRIAGE IS A SOLEMN COVENANT BEFORE GOD AND MAN.

Christian circles commonly refer to marriage as a contract. There's nothing wrong with labeling it that way.[12] This means it's a binding agreement, with reciprocal rights and obligations. However, in modern times, the term "covenant" serves better. It avoids some of the baggage of today's "contracts" (including manipulative clauses and fine print to undermine the contract). It also connects us back to the biblical idea of witnesses to covenants, who hold the covenanting parties accountable to fulfilling them.

Christians have historically understood that those witnesses should

---

11 This is explained very well by A.A. Hodge in *The Westminster Confession: A Commentary* (Carlisle: The Banner of Truth Trust, 2002), 303. (Originally 1869)

12 See for example Hodge, *The Westminster Confession*, 302.

include other people. In the matrimonial ceremony in the Book of Common Prayer,[13] the congregation is called upon to witness the vows. Most of us have guests at our weddings. In many states, marriages have to be witnessed to be legally recognized. But the most important marital witness is God.[14] As Malachi admonished faithless Hebrew husbands, "the Lord was witness between you and the wife of your youth . . . she is your companion and your wife by covenant" (2:14).

When we pledge marital fidelity to the person we're marrying, before God and others, this must not be taken lightly. As Ecclesiastes warns, "It is better that you should not vow than that you should vow and not pay" (5:5). God takes the marriage covenant seriously. He'll honor us doing the same, and judge our unrepentant refusal to uphold it.

6. MARRIAGE IS THE UNION OF TWO AS ONE FLESH.

Perhaps the most important and unique defining reality of marriage is that it's the only human relationship in which a man and a woman become one flesh. Everything else points to this reality—the covenant, the complementary union of male and female, the sex act, the witnessing and involvement of God in joining the partners, and monogamy.

This is laid out foundationally in Genesis 2:21–24:

> So the Lord God caused a deep sleep to fall upon the man, and while he slept took one of his ribs and closed up its place with flesh. And the rib that the Lord God had taken from the man he made into a woman and brought her to the man. Then the man said, 'This at

---

13 313–314.

14 See for example Gordon P. Hugenberger, *Marriage as a Covenant: Biblical Law and Ethics as Developed from Malachi*, (Eugene: Wipf & Stock, 1994), 168.

last is *bone of my bones and flesh of my flesh*; she shall be called Woman, because she was taken out of Man.' Therefore a man shall leave his father and his mother and hold fast to his wife, and *they shall become one flesh*. (Emphases added.)

Jesus points to this historical reality in establishing the foundation of our Christian understanding of marriage. He swept away the concessions and misperceptions of the Jews of his day and pointed us back to creation itself, to marriage's original design and purpose:

> And Pharisees came up to him and tested him by asking, "Is it lawful to divorce one's wife for any cause?" He answered, "Have you not read that he who created them from the beginning made them male and female, and said, 'Therefore a man shall leave his father and his mother and hold fast to his wife, and the two shall become one flesh'? So they are no longer two but one flesh. What therefore God has joined together, let not man separate." (Matt. 19:3–6; see also Mark 10:2–9)

The details surrounding Eve's creation and marriage to Adam are revealing: God took Eve from Adam's side, not from the dust as he had Adam. Then he joined Eve to Adam again. He took of the one and made two, and then in marriage, he united the two as one.

This reality should inform every aspect of our marital relationships. We're to love one another as our own flesh. We're to view divorce as a tragic rending of this one flesh. We're to view our time and our earthly substance as belonging to our spouse as much as to ourselves. This is the foundation for transparency and mutual accountability in marriage. Biblical marital ethics often flow explicitly from marriage as one flesh (see Mal. 2:15–16; Eph. 5:28–31).

7. MARRIAGE REPRESENTS AND EMBODIES THE RELATIONSHIP OF CHRIST AND HIS CHURCH.

This leads naturally into the last reality about marriage as God designed it that I wish to address in this chapter, which I also touched on in the introduction. Marriage represents, and even embodies, the relationship of God to his people, of Christ to his church. As such, godly marriage is a stable witness to the world of the very nature of God as he relates to his people. This profound reality is further connected to the fact that marriage partners are truly one flesh. As we are joined to Christ in his body, the church, so the husband is joined to the wife as one flesh. This isn't just an analogy or a metaphor.

Ephesians 5:22–33 is perhaps the key text on this in the New Testament:

> Wives, submit to your own husbands, as to the Lord. For the husband is the head of the wife even as Christ is the head of the church, his body, and is himself its Savior. Now as the church submits to Christ, so also wives should submit in everything to their husbands.
>
> Husbands, love your wives, as Christ loved the church and gave himself up for her, that he might sanctify her, having cleansed her by the washing of water with the word, so that he might present the church to himself in splendor, without spot or wrinkle or any such thing, that she might be holy and without blemish. In the same way husbands should love their wives as their own bodies. He who loves his wife loves himself. For no one ever hated his own flesh, but nourishes and cherishes it, just as Christ does the church, because we are members of his body. "Therefore a man shall leave his father and mother and hold fast to his wife, and the two shall become one flesh." This mystery is profound, and I am saying that it refers to

Christ and the church. However, let each one of you love his wife as himself, and let the wife see that she respects her husband.

This idea that God is joined to his people as a husband is joined to his wife is often expressed in the Old Testament, in ways and places too numerous to cover here. Books like Hosea are literally constructed around God as the aggrieved husband of a faithless wife. Idolatry is constantly likened to adultery. On a more positive note, the Bible closes with the marriage of Christ to his now-perfected spotless bride, the church (Rev. 19:6–9; 21:2).

Christian married people are called to something both marvelous and fearful. In our marriages, we're called to have a love like that of Jesus' perfect sacrificial love for his people or the church's pure devotion to Christ. And, though we do so imperfectly, in our marriages we're called to represent the gospel at its most profound level to a watching world. May God give us the grace to do this.

1. What expressive individualist ideas about marriage have you embraced?

2. Knowing that marriage was created by God as something central to the foundation of all human society, what attitudes should we have toward it? How should this motivate us to want to know what the Bible teaches about it?

3. Knowing how important sex is to marriage, how should couples prioritize that aspect of their relationship without making an idol of sexual pleasure?

4. How can we learn, in the uniqueness of our own marriages, to recognize and value the complementarity of the sexes built into God's design?

5. How can we protect monogamy, in all that it means, in our marriages?

6. How can we remind ourselves of our marital vows and, by God's grace, strive to fulfill them not only externally but from the heart?

7. How can we keep in front of us, through the daily grind, a knowledge that our spouses are literally joined to us as our own flesh?

8. How can we, with humility and grace, model Christ and his relationship to his people in our marriages?

WHY WOULD ANYONE GET MARRIED?

CHAPTER TWO

Purpose #1: Legitimate & Holy Sexual Relationship

Our culture is obsessed with and confused about sex. As I address in detail in my book *After the Revolution: Sex and the Single Evangelical*,[1] both problems are now widespread among professing evangelicals. Given the difficulties of living in a hyper-sexualized world, the damaged sexual history of many people today, the effects of past sexual abuse suffered by many, and poor teaching about sex in many churches, it's no wonder that sex is an area of confusion or shame for so many Christian married couples.

Dennis Hollinger describes our culture as suffering from "sexual disorientation." And he accurately locates the ultimate source of the problem: "We are confused [about sex] . . . for one simple reason: we have no clear conception of the meaning of sex."[2] And the meaning of sex isn't found in science or worldly philosophy but in the word of God. We must know the meaning that God, the creator of sex, gave to it.

Until we understand God's design for sex, any rules we have about it— even if they're biblical—"hang in the air." They lack foundation. Those rules will only make sense to us when we see how they express God's design for sex. We need to know why God created sex and made it what it is. Only then can our sexual relationships work in our lives as they

---

1   David Ayers, *After the Revolution: Sex and the Single Evangelical* (Bellingham: Lexham Press, 2022).

2   Dennis Hollinger, *The Meaning of Sex: Christian Ethics and the Moral Life* (Grand Rapids: Baker Academic, 2009).

were designed. Thankfully, the Lord has graciously made these deeper principles known to us in his word.

We've seen that God ordained marriage as a monogamous union of one man and one woman in the beginning (Gen. 1:27–28; 2:24). He's commanded that our sexual desires, thoughts, and actions be restricted to that one person to whom we're united in marriage. The writer of Hebrews says, "Let marriage be held in honor among all, and let the marriage bed be undefiled, for God will judge the sexually immoral and adulterous" (13:4). And Jesus explains that sexual purity is about a lot more than just behavior:

> "You have heard that it was said, 'You shall not commit adultery.' But I say to you that everyone who looks at a woman with lustful intent has already committed adultery with her in his heart. If your right eye causes you to sin, tear it out and throw it away. For it is better that you lose one of your members than that your whole body be thrown into hell." (Matt. 5:27–29)

One of the main purposes of marriage, then, is to give men and women a legitimate, holy, productive, good, and lovely way to fulfill their perfectly legitimate sexual desires.[3] The sexual privileges of marriage aren't given to us grudgingly. As the Hebrews passage says, engaging in sex properly within marriage is honorable and undefiled. The apostle Paul urged married couples to maintain regular sexual relations and each spouse to regard their bodies as belonging to the other (1 Cor. 7:2–5). Sex is the first recorded action of Adam and Eve after the Fall (Gen. 4:1). Sex is enjoyable because, like all God has made, it's good if used as he desires it to be used. In fact, the Song of Solomon is an extended celebration

---

3 This is clearly and tersely expressed in the Westminster Confession of Faith "XXIV. Of Marriage and Divorce" section 2, where it identifies "preventing of uncleanness," citing 1 Corinthians 7:2,9 as one of the three reasons for marriage.

of marital love that treats sex as lovely.

Let's unpack God's purposes for marital sex. Then, we will consider some practical realities and implications of sex in marriage according to God's design.

SEX REPRESENTS AND EMBODIES THE ONE FLESH UNION

In the last chapter, I pointed out the amazing reality upon which all Christian marital ethics rests: The covenant of marriage makes a man and woman one flesh. Sex within marriage profoundly embodies and represents this one flesh reality. As such, it's sacred and set apart for marriage among all human relationships, just as marriage is unique and sacred among all human relationships.

Paul points to the way in which sexual intercourse represents and embodies one flesh in his condemnation of sexual immorality. He makes it clear that this is part of the meaning of the Genesis "one flesh" passage (2:23–24): "Do you not know that he who is joined to a prostitute becomes one flesh with her? For as it is written, 'The two will become one flesh'" (1 Cor. 6:16). Put more positively, Bible scholars agree that sexual intercourse is clearly tied to a one flesh marital union.[4]

The one-flesh reality has implications for how married people are to view their bodies. Just as our bodies belong to Jesus Christ, who purchased us with his own blood, joining us to his body, the church (1 Cor. 6:15–20; Gal. 3:13), so the bodies of a husband and wife each belong to the other. Marital sex is perhaps the most profound and intimate way in which this powerful truth is lived out within our marriages (1 Cor. 7:3–4). Man and

---

4 I address this in greater depth in *Christian Marriage*, 32–33.

woman, united in the covenant of marriage, cleave together and yield their bodies to one another in love. This is beautiful, far more lovely than sex as we see it portrayed in most of modern culture today.

All of this means that sex within marriage is sacred, just as marriage itself is sacred. This doesn't mean that we have to approach it in exaggerated piety or super-spirituality. Sex between a husband and wife is earthy and physical, just as our bodies are. And yet the symbolism of marital sex is deeply spiritual.

MARITAL SEX POINTS TO CHRIST

We also saw in the last chapter that marriage embodies the relationship of Christ and his people in ways that are profound and mysterious (Eph. 5:32). Because it's bound with the one-flesh reality of marriage, sex must inevitably do the same. This means that passages like Ephesians 5:22–33 apply to so much in our marital relationships, including how we approach sex as husbands and wives. Spouses ought to love one another as their own flesh, and their relationship should resemble the relationship between Christ and his church.

Throughout the Bible, God often describes his relationship with his people in marital and sexual terms. Where this is applied to their faithlessness, disloyalty, and fickleness, the sexual language used to illustrate this can be powerful, even disturbing. For example, Jeremiah 2:24 describes the idolatrous Jews as being like wild donkeys in heat. Their going after other gods is often compared to adultery (Hos. 4:12–14; Jer. 3:20; Isa. 57:8; Ezek. 6:9).

But we also see marriage imagery used positively. For example, in sexually suggestive ways, God describes himself with his people as a husband spreading his garment over his wife to cover her nakedness, bathing and anointing her, dressing her with fine clothes and jewelry in Ezekiel 16:8–14. It's an image of a husband who delights in his wife and wants to admire her beauty. This metaphor give us a picture of how a married couple's sexual relationship can image the love between Christ and his church in its tenderness, generosity, and delight. These images not only show the loveliness and goodness that can be realized in the physical relationship between husband and wife rooted in godly mutual love, but also how this reflects deep and enduring spiritual realities.

MARITAL SEX SHOULD BE DELIGHTFUL, BUT NOT SELFISH

All I have just said about sex being one flesh and pointing to Christ as marriage does means that a husband and wife should never become mere objects of sexual gratification for one another. Just as it's wrong to use an unmarried person to gratify our lust, so it is with our spouses. There ought to be mutual consideration, tenderness, sacrificial love, the desire to please and delight the other more than to be served, and so much more in the sexual lives of married Christians. This doesn't mean that it can't and won't be physically delightful. Rather, it means our deepest sexual pleasures will be found in satisfying, honoring, and loving each other.

So much of modern culture is at war with the Christian understanding of marital sex. Exposure to porn, which many men and women have suffered both before and sometimes during marriage, undermines godly marital sex. Casual sex on prime-time television makes selfish ways of thinking about sex as natural to modern people as breathing. This is often carried into their marital relationships. A quest for powerful physical sexual experiences even in marriage can become consuming, leading to sin. For example, many worldly sex manuals encourage couples to enhance their sexual relationships by viewing erotic films together. The powerful orgasm becomes something like the Holy Grail. When this happens, sex is treated not as an act of love that's also pleasurable and fulfilling but as an end in itself. When we do this, sex becomes more like an illicit drug than the beautiful experience God gave married men and women to enjoy.

On the other hand, yes, there ought to be joy in marital sex, even laughter at times, along with many other earthly goods such as comfort and release. The Bible doesn't give us a dour, stingy, only-your-duty view of marital sex. In Genesis, when Abimelech looks out his window, he sees Isaac enjoying what appears to have been some kind of sexual intimacy with Rebekah (which is why he concluded that Rebekah wasn't Isaac's sister). The English Standard Version renders it "laughing with" her, while the King James Version uses the term "sporting" (Gen. 26:8).[5]

The Song of Solomon presents us with powerful sexual desire and anticipation between a groom and his intended bride. In the first chapter alone, we find every one of the senses called upon for this. In fact, in the English Standard Version the subtitle "Solomon and His Bride Delight in Each Other" following verse seven refers to the anticipation of physical, sexual intimacy in marriage. Consider this stunning passage, in which the groom is speaking to the bride:

> How beautiful are your feet in sandals, O noble daughter! Your rounded thighs are like jewels, the work of a master hand. Your navel is a rounded bowl that never lacks mixed wine. Your belly is a heap of wheat, encircled with lilies. Your two breasts are like two fawns, twins of a gazelle. Your neck is like an ivory tower. Your eyes are pools in Heshbon, by the gate of Bath-rabbim. Your nose is like a tower of Lebanon, which looks toward Damascus. Your head crowns

---

5 We sometimes also see "caressing" in various translations.

you like Carmel, and your flowing locks are like purple; a king is held captive in the tresses. How beautiful and pleasant you are, O loved one, with all your delights! Your stature is like a palm tree, and your breasts are like its clusters. I say I will climb the palm tree and lay hold of its fruit. Oh may your breasts be like clusters of the vine, and the scent of your breath like apples, and your mouth like the best wine. (7:1–9)

The Puritans are often viewed as cheerless people who wouldn't have encouraged the enjoyment of marital sex as something good in itself. Nothing could be further from the truth. One Puritan minister said that, in sex, husband and wife should "joyfully give due benevolence one to another; as two musical instruments rightly fitted to make a most pleasant and sweet harmony in a well-tuned consort." Another urged that sex in marriage should be enjoyed with "good will and delight, willingly, readily, and cheerfully."[6] Both gave excellent pastoral advice.

MARITAL SEX CAN BE A FORM OF COMFORT

Along with many joys and blessings, life in a fallen world brings many sources of grief and sorrow. As we will see further in the next chapter and we touched on in the last, marriage is a source of strength and support in such times. It's a bulwark against loneliness as well, a source of intimate companionship that, in a good marriage, is steady and reliable.

Though we rarely think about it this way, marital sex can be part of the means by which a husband and wife provide comfort to each other. This is something we find often in talking to people who have been married

---

6   Both quoted in Leland Ryken, *Worldly Saints: The Puritans as They Really Were* (Grand Rapids: Zondervan, 1986), 44.

for a long time. Psychologists have known this for years.[7]

This is at least part of what we find going on in one of the most beautiful love stories in the Bible—the story of Isaac and Rebekah. "Then Isaac brought her into the tent of Sarah his mother and took Rebekah, and she became his wife, and he loved her. So Isaac was comforted after his mother's death" (Gen. 24:67).

We see this in less dramatic ways in day-to-day married life. Sex to alleviate anxiety. Sex even as a way to relax together and usher each other into slumber. The close physical intimacy and release that comes from sex can sometimes be like medicine. It's one of the ways that husbands and wives help one another through the rough roads of life.

MARITAL SEX IS FOR A LIFETIME

When Paul encouraged married saints to maintain a regular sex life (1 Cor. 7:3–5), he didn't set an age limit. We don't find here or anywhere in the Bible that marital sex must end with old age.

That said, it's certainly true that beyond a certain age, it's normal for sex drives to cool. Sexual relationships between married persons become less frequent as they enter old age, and most couples are perfectly happy with this. Still, there are a lot of misperceptions, and there's a lot of room for variation among couples as they age. For example, in the *General Social Survey* over the last decade combined, over 68 percent of married people ages 60 to 69 had sex at least monthly, with 21 percent doing so two or three times a month and a quarter doing so

---

7 See for example Stephanie A. Sarkis, "5 Things They Don't Tell You About Grieving," *Psychology Today*, November 23, 2015, https://www.psychologytoday.com/us/blog/here-there-and-everywhere/201511/5-things-they-dont-tell-you-about-grief. The problem with psychological advice about this is that most don't affirm that sex is appropriate for coping with grief only within marriage.

weekly or more. Among those in their 70's, well over half had sex monthly or more often, with almost 30 percent doing so two to three times per month or more often. Even after 80, many couples still have sex, about 35 percent monthly or more.

All that said, this isn't a contest nor is it right to judge your own sex life relative to any such statistical benchmarks. There isn't a right or wrong amount of sex for married people at any age if both are content and not neglecting this aspect of their marriage unnecessarily. Regular sex should be a part of most marriages through most of a couple's life together, though what that means can legitimately vary across marriages.

Certainly, serious illness and disability can put an end to sex altogether. Advanced age makes that a lot more likely. There may sometimes be other situations that prevent sex for very long periods of time, as may occur with military duty or, among the persecuted, imprisonment. Some people may become too old and frail for sex. Although such difficulties may bring sex to a halt, it should never mean that sexual *faithfulness* or the marital covenant itself ends. The vows we made at marriage are for as long as both shall live, no matter what terrible events overtake us. At such times, if a remaining spouse continues to desire sex, God will give them the grace to be faithful to their vows.

MARITAL SEX IS INTEGRALLY RELATED TO MARITAL HAPPINESS

We social scientists have known for a long time that a healthy, regular sex life is associated with higher marital happiness. This is as we would expect from the Scriptures. God knit marriage with sex by design, placed it at the core of marriage, and made it pleasurable and unifying. Thus, the sexual relationship will contribute positively to the marital one.

He also made the marital bond ideally and naturally a deep, mutually supportive companionship between a man and a woman. It stands to reason that to the extent that husbands and wives love, serve, and enjoy the company of one another, they will not only be happier in general and in their marriage, but they will also more readily embrace sexual relations.

So, when I demonstrate that regular sex and marital happiness are statistically related to each other, I'm often asked, "Is it sex that leads to marital happiness, or marital happiness that leads to sex?" My reply is, "Yes." The relationship between these two things is mutual. In the *General Social Survey* for the last decade this is clear. Among married people, as sexual frequency increases, the percentages that say their marriage is "very happy" also rises dramatically. This holds for older age groups, not just those who are younger.

EVERY MARRIED COUPLE HAS SEXUAL UPS AND DOWNS

Over the course of any marriage, a couple will experience periods of difficulty in their sex life, just as they will in other aspects of their marriage. Illness, pregnancy, childbirth, living with newborns, stress and exhaustion, and the impact of medication and surgery are among many obvious reasons a couple may have "down times" sexually. There will be disagreements about sex just as there will be about so much else. Communication, compromise, commitment, and love will normally see couples through those times. Considering how relational issues outside of sex may be impacting the quality of a couple's sexual relationship is critical. Knowing that such periods are normal helps too.

If and when a couple needs to seek education and counseling for extraordinary sexual difficulties, sometimes beyond what their pastor or others in their life are able to provide, they will need to pursue this with care.

Most sexual "experts," whatever good they might do, approach sex from a worldly perspective, and may provide instruction and advice contrary to biblical morals. Many so-called Christian counselors are not much better. Investigate any prospective sexual helper thoroughly, and don't settle for anyone who is not committed to a biblical sexual ethic.

WHEN THE GOING GETS REALLY TOUGH

As in other areas of marriage, some sexual problems may be rooted in deep-seated and complex realities that defy easy answers, even from sound, biblical counselors. What help is there for people who struggle with shame, perhaps about their bodies, perhaps relative to some earlier sexual trauma or abuse? What about believers struggling to be faithful spouses, including sexually, in unions that are deeply unhappy, perhaps with partners who are selfish, emotionally distant, or even abusive? What happens when these problems go on for a long time? Another common area of difficulty is spouses who make inappropriate or uncomfortable sexual demands. These kinds of issues seem to be increasingly common due to the expressive individualism of our culture and the expectations fueled by exposure to pornography.

In a fallen world in which every marriage involves two sinful human beings, often with broken sexual histories, these kinds of issues will come up in many Christian marriages. Like any powerful, central aspect of God's creation, sex that is misused can do great damage. Lisa Fullam's observations are accurate, even for Christian married couples: "Sex can be everything from a . . . transaction without emotional meaning, to a profound experience of loving union . . . Sex can be tender or violently abusive; it can heal and deeply wound."[8] There isn't space here to provide detailed

---

8   As quoted in Hollinger's *The Meaning of Sex*, 12.

counsel on this difficult range of issues, but I hope the following will help.

First, it's important to rely on, remember, and apply the core teachings of the gospel to the sexual challenges we face in marriage. For both you and your spouse, "the law of the Spirit has set you free in Christ Jesus from the law of sin and death" (Rom. 8:2). For both you and your spouse, "he who began a good work in you will bring it to completion at the day of Jesus Christ" (Phil. 1:6). For the guilt so many of us have over our sexual pasts: "as far as the east is from the west, so far does he remove our transgressions from us" (Ps. 103:12). The same grace to love and forgive that we enjoy from God can, by his grace, be exercised toward our spouses.

Reviewing 1 Corinthians 13 on the attributes of true love can also be helpful for spouses struggling sexually. This can be true for both parties, but especially for the spouse being selfish and demanding. After all, love is "patient and kind," not "arrogant or rude." It "does not insist on its own way," neither is it "irritable or resentful" (v. 4–5). If I can't forego something I want that my spouse tells me he or she finds harmful or offensive—even if it's not clearly sinful to me—how does this square with biblical love? Conversely, at times the compromise will go in the other direction, as when one partner accepts the sexual advances of the other even when he or she is not "in the mood." If *both* partners are committed to loving each other in ways consistent with true biblical love, many differences can be worked out.

Next, it's important not to go it alone. We're not designed to walk out any aspect of our Christian lives, including our marriages and sexual relationships, by ourselves. Jesus has placed us into his body, the church (1 Cor. 12:12, 27; Rom. 12:4–5). He's given us pastors, elders, trusted friends, and older saints. They can encourage us, pray for us, advise us, even help us sit down with our spouses for difficult conversations. We must not hesitate to avail ourselves of this kind of help, especially when things seem impossible or have hit a dead end.

As Hollinger notes, many sexual issues plaguing married couples simply require better communication skills.[9] We may just need help improving these. Fortunately, good teaching and training focused on improving marital communication is widely available. Competent counselors, pastors, and marriage mentors can help couples with this.

Meanwhile, commit your marriage and your sex life to God, the one who designed both. He's faithful and delights in the godly sexual relationships of his people in marriage. He who saved you by his own blood won't abandon or forsake you (Heb. 13:5).

---

9 Hollinger, *The Meaning of Sex*, 153.

1. What difference does it make to the way Christian married couples approach sex to understand how it expresses a one-flesh relationship that reflects the relationship of Christ and his people?

2. What are some practical ways that husbands and wives can desire sex with their spouses, and express those desires, without becoming demanding, manipulative, or otherwise selfish?

3. How can married people look after each other's sexual needs as part of their overall care for their spouses?

4. How can married couples enjoy each other's bodies sexually, using all their senses, without this becoming lurid or lustful?

5. How and why might marital sex have therapeutic effects, such as providing comfort in grief or providing respite from the stresses of life?

6. Is it surprising that older, married saints usually continue to enjoy sexual relationships?

7. In what ways do you see, practically, marital happiness and regular, healthy sexual relationships each contributing to the other over the course of a marriage?

8. What kinds of conversations might married couples need to have if they're struggling in their sexual relationship?

9. When do spouses, individually or as couples, need to reach out for help? To whom should they turn?

CHAPTER THREE

Purpose #2: Mutual Help & Companionship

Our culture is in the middle of a loneliness epidemic. A Harvard University report released in 2021 documented this problem, now being made worse by the COVID-19 pandemic. There's a "wide hole in our social fabric" that has been worsening for some time.[1]

Sharp increases in the number of people describing themselves as lonely is a terrible and destructive trend with many causes. But paramount among them is the flight from committed, covenant marriage. As this report shows, never married, divorced, and separated adults are struggling with loneliness far more than those who are married.[2] Meanwhile, the last decade of the *General Social Survey* (*GSS*) shows that married adults are much more likely to be "very" happy, and more importantly, dramatically *less* likely to be unhappy. This is true in every level of education and social class. This would not be the case if married adults were suffering from loneliness at similar rates as others.

These trends of increasing loneliness coincide with plummeting marriage rates, which are the lowest we've ever seen.[3] Census data shows that

---

1   Richard Weissbourd, et al, *Loneliness in America: How the Pandemic Has Deepened an Epidemic of Loneliness and What We Can Do About It*, February 8, 2021, 12. Harvard Graduate School of Education, Making Caring Common Project, https://static1.squarespace.com/static/5b7c56e255b02c683659fe43/t/6021776bd-d04957c4557c212/1612805995893/Loneliness+in+America+2021_02_08_FINAL.pdf.

2   Weissbourd, *Loneliness in America*, 8.

3   Lydia Anderson and Zachary Scherer, "U.S. Marriage and Divorce Rates Declined in the Last Ten Years," December 7, 2020, United States Census Bureau, https://www.census.gov/library/stories/2020/12/united-states-marriage-and-divorce-rates-declined-last-10-years.html.

new marriages per all unmarried women ages 15 and older in 2018 were almost two and a half times lower compared to 1970.[4]

Divorce has been declining, but this isn't helping much. Why not? Because much of this decrease results from there being fewer marriages to begin with, especially as we go down the economic ladder. A rapidly growing share of those who are married are affluent. They're a lot less likely to get divorced compared to those who are less well off.[5]

Meanwhile, declining or not, divorce is still high. The Centers for Disease Control and Prevention (CDC) estimated that, for women ages 15 through 44 in 2011 through 2015, 45 percent of all first marriages would be disrupted by divorce, separation, or death[6] within 15 years of their wedding.[7] Marital breakdown may be going down, but it's still alarmingly common.

In our current cultural moment—with high divorce and low marriage fueling epidemic loneliness—it's important to highlight the wonderful fact that God has designed marriage to provide mutual help and companionship. Committed, godly marriages are a blessing and support through the ups and downs of life. We need to treasure this and understand what it means more than ever as people increasingly abandon marriage.

---

4 Comparing 1970 figure from *The State of Our Unions Marriage in America 2012: The President's Marriage Agenda for the Forgotten Sixty Percent* (Charlottesville: The National Marriage Project, 2012), 63, with the comparable 2018 figure from Valerie Schweizer, "First Marriage Rates in the U.S., 2018," *Family Profile* No. 20, 01, Bowling Green State University: National Center for Marriage and Family Research, https://www.bgsu.edu/ncfmr/resources/data/family-profiles/schweizer-first-marriage-rate-fp-20-01.html.

5 Richard V. Reeves and Christopher Pulliam, "Middle Class Marriage is Declining, and Likely Deepening Inequality," The Brookings Institute Future of the Middle Class Initiative. March 11, 2020. https://www.brookings.edu/research/middle-class-marriage-is-declining-and-likely-deepening-inequality/. W. Bradford Wilcox and Wendy Wang, "The Marriage Divide: How and Why Working-Class Families are More Fragile Today," American Enterprise Institute, September 25, 2017, https://www.aei.org/research-products/report/the-marriage-divide-how-and-why-working-class-families-are-more-fragile-today/.

6 Death, however, is rare for this age group.

7 "Key Statistics from the National Survey of Family Growth - D Listing," National Center for Health Statistics, The Centers for Disease Control and Prevention, https://www.cdc.gov/nchs/nsfg/key_statistics/d.htm.

Yes, God also provides for the unmarried, especially through his people: "God sets the solitary in a home" said the Psalmist (68:6a), a promise he gives to us regardless of our marital status. Moreover, marriage is not, nor should it ever be, our sole source of interpersonal support and companionship. God has made us part of his body (1 Cor. 12:12–27) and admonishes us to regularly worship and fellowship with the saints (Heb. 10:25). The apostle Paul himself, along with many believers throughout history, are testimony to the fact that the unmarried have access to a fulfilling and productive place in the Kingdom.

Nevertheless, for most adults, marriage is a vital provision for our mutual help and companionship. This aspect of marriage is central for God's plan for humanity, including our properly exercising stewardship over the earth. In Genesis 2:18, we find God saying, prior to the creation of Eve, "It is not good that the man should be alone; I will make him a helper fit for him." Genesis 1:26–27 had already directed the "male and female he created" to "rule over" every living thing. We know that the beginning of all of this was Adam and Eve, husband and wife, united as one flesh by God himself.

Let's explore more deeply the nature and benefits of marriage as mutual help and companionship, and what specific marital characteristics tend to increase these blessings. We will also, as we did in the last chapter, recognize that sometimes things go wrong and consider godly ways for responding to that.

THE AMAZING BENEFITS OF MARRIAGE

Social science has stockpiled a lot of solid research over the years documenting the benefits of marriage that certainly fit what we would expect to see given its purposes set forth in Genesis. These studies set apart marriage not only from singleness, divorce, and separation, but also from the cheap alternative known as cohabitation. I don't have space here to get into detail on every one of these benefits, but we can do a quick overview.[8]

I've already touched on the fact that married people are happier and less prone to loneliness. This alone reduces the risks for "early mortality and a wide array of serious physical and emotional problems, including depression, anxiety, heart disease, substance abuse, and domestic abuse."[9] But these are only some of the benefits associated with marriage.

Married people are less likely to commit suicide. They have better overall physical health that shows up in being less likely to contract, and more likely to recover from or successfully manage, a range of serious ailments. Moreover, married people discourage each other from engaging in destructive and dangerous behavior, while encouraging healthy practices such as getting enough exercise and sleep. They are more likely to survive cardiac surgery, heart attacks, and cancer. All of this shows the practical support that spouses give each other.

I've seen dramatic improvement from my own diagnosis of coronary artery disease over twenty years ago. My wife played a major role in encouraging me to do everything I was supposed to in order to manage my condition.

Marriage is also helpful financially. It motivates earning, saving, and frugality, and provides shared resources. Married people earn more, invest more, and save more.

---

8 For this, see David Ayers, *Christian Marriage: A Comprehensive Introduction* (Bellingham: Lexham Press, 2018), 48–54.

9 Weissbourd, *Loneliness in America*, 1, 3.

This cornucopia of marital benefits is wonderful and clearly points to the mutual help and companionship that marriage makes possible. Yet if we're honest and observant, we see many marriages that don't seem to live up to this rosy picture. Why not? Why do some married people see these benefits of mutual help and companionship, and others do not, or at least see far less of them?

MUTUAL HELP AND COMPANIONSHIP AREN'T GUARANTEED

Like the other two purposes of marriage, mutual help and companionship and their many benefits aren't promised to us independent of how we choose to live as husband and wife. This requires effort supported and motivated by the grace of God and the teachings of Scripture and faithful churches, and we'll always fall short.

Were this not so, Paul's marvelous teaching about the characteristics of godly spouses in Ephesians 5:22–33 would be unnecessary. Given all that Christ has done for us, given that marriage is the union of man and woman as one flesh serving as witness to the mystical union of Christ and the church, says Paul, strive by God's grace to live like this. And the attitude and motivations he describes here—respect, love, caring for your spouse as you care for yourself, and so on—add up to mutual help and companionship. We have the promise and the potential, but realizing it in our marriages is something we must seek to do across the span of our lives together.

This is sometimes stated negatively in the Bible. Such Proverbs as 12:4, 19:13, and 21:9 make this clear. The Scriptures are full of examples of poor marriages that tear people down rather than build them up. To name just one, consider the marriage of Abigail to the churlish and ridiculous man Nabal described in 1 Samuel 25. Social science research has likewise shown that the quality of marital relationships is critical to realizing the benefits of marriage.[10]

THE KEY FACTORS OF A GOOD MARRIAGE

In an excellent 2011 report, the National Marriage Project at the University of Virginia summarized the key factors associated with such good, happy marriages.[11] Their findings about things that characterize good marriages correspond powerfully with the teachings of Scripture. All married couples can improve on these things:

One stand-out factor is sound money management.[12] This is widely acknowledged in social science literature. It's critically important to avoid excessive debt. Key to doing so is curbing our appetites and resisting the materialism and consumerism of our age. Heavy debt introduces stress and conflict, undermining marital relationships. Sometimes, serious money problems happen through no fault of our own. However, we should avoid bringing them upon ourselves. The writer of Hebrews encourages us not to love money and to be content with what we have, rooted in the sufficiency of Christ (13:5).

Simply taking on the burdens of household duties equitably goes a long way.[13] When it comes to chores and childcare, both spouses need to pull their weight, neither taking advantage of the other. This has nothing to do with the old debate about sex-typed assignments, such as women

---

10 Ayers, *Christian Marriage*, 51.

11 *The State of Our Unions 2011: When Baby Makes Three: How Parenthood Makes Life Meaningful and How Marriage Makes Parenthood Bearable*. ed. W. Bradford Wilcox (Charlottesville, VA: The National Marriage Project and the Institute for American Values, 2011), 17–47.

12 *When Baby Makes Three*, 20–22.

13 *When Baby Makes Three*, 22–24.

changing diapers and men raking the lawn. It's about serving and caring for one another and for your families, equally.

Next, we have the critical role played by the support of family and friends. The best marriages exist within a rich tapestry of supportive relationships. The opposite is true as well. Negative, unsupportive friends and family members operate upon marriage like poison.[14] Married couples should seek out and draw near to friends and family who support godly marriage. Meanwhile, they ought to avoid or carefully manage personal relationships that are negative influences upon them.

My wife and I knew a married couple years ago in which the wife got involved in a tight circle of married women that spent a lot of time talking about what was wrong with their husbands. Her husband meanwhile threw himself into his work friends, who likewise did little to encourage him in his marriage. There were real problems beyond this but no way they could fix them while embedded in these toxic peer relationships. Within less than a year of us noticing this, they were divorced and raising their two children in single parent households.

Regular church attendance is powerfully and positively associated with marital quality. Spouses agreeing that "God is at the center of our marriage" is tied to stronger, happier unions even more. Neither of these should surprise us, given the clear admonishments of Scripture that we regularly meet with fellow saints, encouraging one another (Heb. 10:25) and that we keep God central in *every* aspect of our lives (1 Cor. 10:31).[15]

Next, they found that couples who have more traditional beliefs about family and marriage, which more often align with Scripture, have happier marriages. One key attribute is being opposed to easy divorce,

---

14 *When Baby Makes Three*, 26–30.

15 *When Baby Makes Three*, 30–32.

believing that troubled married couples should try to work through their problems and not simply walk away. Another is valuing children.[16] Given Jesus' teaching about divorce (Matt. 19:3–12; Mark 10:2–12) and children (Matt. 19:13–14), this means having biblical, godly attitudes toward our marital vows and our children.

As we discussed in the last chapter, sexual satisfaction is also important to a strong and healthy marriage. The authors note that there will be times that regular sex is hard: for example, after childbirth. But couples should return sexual frequency to normal when they can.[17]

The next two factors that this report addresses are extremely important. In fact, they both contribute mightily, or are otherwise tied to, the factors I have already covered.

The first of these is simple generosity toward one another.[18] This means small acts of kindness and affection, the regular practice of forgiveness, and showing respect. There's nothing mechanical about this. It's "giving good things . . . freely and abundantly" out of a willing heart.[19] What could capture better the essence of Ephesians 5:22–33? How hard is it to find in Scripture that we're called to treat others this way generally, but especially our spouses? How could a marriage marked by two individuals displaying these qualities not be happy? And isn't it easy to see why generous couples have better sex lives?

Then we have commitment.[20] I love how the authors define this. Commitment isn't just mechanically keeping vows, important as that

---

16 *When Baby Makes Three*, 32–34.
17 *When Baby Makes Three*, 35–37.
18 *When Baby Makes Three*, 38.
19 *When Baby Makes Three*, 38.
20 *When Baby Makes Three*, 35–37.

is, but:

> the extent to which spouses see their relationship in terms of "we" versus "me," the importance they attach to their relationship, their conviction that a better relationship with someone else does not exist, and their desire to stay in the relationship "no matter what rough times we encounter."[21]

Finally, the authors note something that's obvious but so often neglected: time. Couples need time alone together. When they have children, they also need to have time together as a family. Moreover, when mothers and fathers spend time with their children, this is also tied to better marriage.[22] Modern life is full of busyness and distraction. Married people need to prioritize time with their families, their children, and each other. Marriage is a relationship. Relationships take time.

Before I move on to the next section, I'd like to focus on two other relational factors we know are critical to marital quality. In fact, virtually every sound approach to pre-marital and marital counseling and education addresses these, including practical training. I'm talking about communication and conflict resolution skills. These are connected. Every problem that can come up in marriage is aggravated when these skills are lacking. Meanwhile, every aspect of marriage is enhanced when couples can do these well. And there's always room for improvement.

Marital relationships are more art than science. The process of learning to communicate clearly and affectionately, knowing each other deeply, will unfold over a lifetime. Disagreements will happen. In fact, this is often healthy. If we're honestly sharing our thoughts—and our failings, mistakes, and sins—won't this lead to different points of view and, at

---

21 *When Baby Makes Three*, 42.

22 *When Baby Makes Three*, 44–47.

times, tension? The best marriages aren't free of conflict, and they're certainly not characterized by avoiding necessary conflict. Instead, in good marriages the partners remain committed to each other in spite of their differences and work through them constructively. Marriage retreats and workshops, counseling, good books on marital communication—there are lots of great resources out there that can help married couples do this better. Any marriage can benefit from these.

FRIENDS BUT MORE THAN FRIENDS

In a good marriage, each spouse is the other's dearest friend. This should be the closest relationship each person has. A godly marriage has the qualities of what Aristotle categorized as the highest and noblest type of friendship—one in which the friends want to see each other develop virtue or moral goodness. They should be jealous to see one another grow in holiness.

Yet marriage goes well beyond friendship. Marriage and friendship are different in many important ways. Friends can be of the same sex. Many friendships revolve around a small set of common activities or shared passions. They aren't exclusive in the way marriage is. Having more than one close friend, or a close-knit group of friends, is perfectly normal. Friendships can cool and end without any grave sin or violation of covenants.

It's important to remember too, as I touched on above, that married people do need healthy friendships outside their marriage. Sound marriages are embedded in a web of supportive friendships, including "couple friends," but also people that the husband and the wife each maintain friendships with individually.

WHAT ABOUT THOSE IN MARRIAGES MARKED BY ALIENATION OR ABUSE?

Many of you reading this are in marriages marked by loneliness, neglect, emotional abandonment, and chronic anger. Some of you are experiencing seemingly endless conflicts in which the party who is obviously wrong about important matters that must be resolved never admits or corrects it. Marriages can be marred by verbal or physical abuse. To you, much that I'm saying here may sound hollow.

It may be that the hope of having a marriage that fulfills God's ideal purposes of mutual support and companionship seems to be for others, but not for you. Sadly, I've known too many believers in marriages that stopped being even a minimally satisfying relationship years ago.

Let me begin by emphasizing the importance of your safety. Where there's serious physical risk and abuse, involving oneself or children, it may be necessary to physically separate prior to any counseling being sought. I was in a church where one married woman had to do that, and the pastors and congregation supported her and her family completely. Where crime has been committed, those helping shouldn't hesitate to report this to the proper authorities.

Much of what you need to keep in mind—the hope of the gospel, the constancy and love of the Lord for you, the need to find support in prayer and godly counsel—I touched on in the last chapter. That is to say, again, I won't insult you with easy answers or cheap promises.

However, there are some encouraging facts revealed in sound social science research, in addition to what I've already said. These insights apply particularly to deeply unhappy marriages where abuse and infidelity haven't occurred.[23]

The vast majority of marriages that come unglued aren't characterized by high levels of conflict, abuse, or adultery. Most problems are resolvable, if both partners are willing to recommit to and invest in the marriage. In fact, in one major study, two-thirds of married people who said their marriage was "unhappy" but who chose to stick with and work on it, identified their marital union as "happy" five years later. Their five-year outcomes were far superior to those who, though similar in their levels of unhappiness at the beginning, chose to give up on their marriages.

What's key for many who persevere and see their marriages redeemed, even made wonderful, out of these dark times? First, they plug into a sound, local church and drink in the support offered there. They also likely pray and read and meditate upon the Scriptures.

They may also seek sound marriage counseling. One key element in such counseling is being committed to the institution of marriage in general and to saving your marriage in particular. Avoid marriage counselors who claim to be "value-neutral" with regard to divorce. Find someone skilled in helping improve communication and conflict resolution skills. Counselors should also identify and help resolve underlying issues that place strain on marriages such as financial mismanagement. And where there are serious sin issues on the part of one or both partners—such as explosive anger, use of pornography, and substance abuse—they shouldn't hesitate to identify that as sin, encourage repentance, and get skilled additional help as needed. Above all, don't lose heart. Remember, "he who has called you is faithful" (1 Thess. 5:24a).

---

23 The insights that follow are drawn from my article, "Unhappily Married or Happily Divorced? The False Dilemma," *Modern Reformation*, January 25, 2021, https://modernreformation.org/resource-library/web-exclusive-articles/the-mod-unhappily-married-or-happily-divorced-the-false-dilemma/.

DISCUSSION QUESTIONS

1. How much are modern people suffering from rising levels of loneliness and its fruits? How is this connected partially to the breakdown of the institution of marriage?

2. Theologians have agreed that mutual support and companionship is a basic purpose God has given to marriage. Does that mean we have an unconditional promise that our marriages will provide us with good support and companionship?

3. How and why can keeping sound finances and avoiding greed help keep your marriage strong?

4. What does a marriage look like in which the daily work of maintaining a household and family is shared equally? Why are such couples usually happier?

5. In what ways have you seen the "right" kinds of influences from family members and friends help marriages? Conversely, in what ways have you seen the "wrong" kind of family members and friends hurt them? What are some strategies for building up the right influences and avoiding or managing the wrong ones?

6. What are your core beliefs about your marital vows? How about the role and importance of children? Upon what are these beliefs based?

7. Identify a number of ways that generosity to your spouse can be exhibited, each of which requires little or no money.

8. What does it mean to you to be committed to your marriage? What are some practical ways this can be demonstrated?

9. What pressures and enticements of modern life lead people to spend less time with their spouses and families then they should?

10. In what ways do good skills in communication and handling conflict improve every aspect of marriage? How can serious deficiencies in these areas make every other problem worse and harder to solve?

11. How important is your friendship with your spouse? Is it marked by a desire to see their highest good as someone seeking to grow in Christ?

12. What practical encouragement can we take from the experience of those in unhappy marriages who choose to remain committed to their marriages?

13. What should couples look for in a counselor if they decide they need intervention because their marriage has become deeply unhappy?

CHAPTER FOUR

Purpose #3: Procreation & Child Rearing

Both having children and raising them within healthy marriages are dramatically declining in modern societies. The United States is no exception. In 2019, American fertility rates were the lowest in recorded history, far below replacement level.[1] Meanwhile, recent polling by Pew Research Institute revealed that having an enjoyable job and career was between more than three and a half (men) and two (females) times more likely to be seen as "essential to a fulfilling life" compared to having children. Almost 30 percent of both men and women considered children to be totally unimportant to a having fulfilling life, compared to between 3 (men) and 5 (women) percent saying the same thing about enjoyable jobs and careers.[2] Topping that off, a large percentage of childless adults ages 18 to 49 now say they're unlikely to ever have children—44 percent, up from 37 percent in 2018. Most of those unlikely to have children say they simply don't want them.[3]

Providing children with married parents is also increasingly less important to people. In America, about four in ten births, and the majority of

---

1   Joyce A. Martin et al., "Births: Final Data for 2019," *National Vital Statistics Report*, Volume 70, no. 2 (March 23, 2021): 14.

2   Amanda Barroso, "More Than Half of Americans Say Marriage is Important but Not Essential to Leading a Fulfilling Life," *Pew Research Center*, February 14, 2020, https://www.pewresearch.org/fact-tank/2020/02/14/more-than-half-of-americans-say-marriage-is-important-but-not-essential-to-leading-a-fulfilling-life/.

3   Anna Brown, "Growing Share of Childless Adults In U.S. Don't Expect To Ever Have Children," *Pew Research Center*, November 19, 2021, https://www.pewresearch.org/fact-tank/2021/11/19/growing-share-of-childless-adults-in-u-s-dont-expect-to-ever-have-children/.

births to women under the age of 30, are now out-of-wedlock.[4] Yes, most of such births take place within cohabiting unions.[5] Yet children in these households are about twice as likely as those in married ones to see their parents break up.[6] Currently, about one in three children under 18 do not live with both their parents, married or otherwise. This is up from only about 10 percent in 1960.[7] Most American children will live with someone other than their two married parents by the time they're 18.

There are many negative results. Let's look at one crucially important one—suicide among children. This was almost unknown when sociologist Emile Durkheim wrote his treatise *Suicide* in 1897. As of 2017, it was the third leading cause of death among children ages 10 to 14 and the tenth among those in elementary school.[8] Child suicide rates have continued to rise sharply, at least through 2020.[9] According to the CDC's Youth Risk Behavior Survey, in 2019, almost one in ten high school kids had attempted suicide in the previous year. About 3 percent required medical treatment as a result. About one in five seriously considered suicide. What could lead so many children and youth to this level of despair?[10] Doesn't this tell us something about the unhealthy environments too many of our children are being raised in?

---

4   Martin et al., "Births: Final Data for 2019," 6; Jason Deparle and Sabrina Tavernise, "For Women Under 30, Most Births Occur Outside Marriage," *New York Times*, February 18, 2012, https://www.nytimes.com/2012/02/18/us/for-women-under-30-most-births-occur-outside-marriage.html.

5   Sally C. Curtin, Stephanie J. Ventura, and Gladys M. Martinez, "Recent Declines in Nonmarital Childbearing in the United States," *National Center for Health Statistics Data Brief*, no. 162 (August 2014, 4): http://www.cdc.gov/nchs/data/databriefs/db162.pdf.

6   Wilcox, W. Bradford, and Laurie DeRose, "In Europe, Cohabitation is Stable...Right?," *Brookings Institute*, March 27, 2017, https://www.brookings.edu/blog/social-mobility-memos/2017/03/27/in-europe-cohabitation-is-stable-right/.

7   2021 statistics calculated from "Living Arrangements of Children Under 18: 1960—2021," *Historical Living Arrangements of Children*, U.S. Census., November 2021, https://www.census.gov/data/tables/time-series/demo/families/children.html.

8   Curley, Bob, "Why Are So Many Young Children Killing Themselves?," *Healthline*, August 31, 2017, https://www.healthline.com/health-news/why-are-young-children-killing-themselves.

9   Gartx, Micha, "More 'Covid Suicides' Than Covid Deaths in Kids," *American Institute for Economic Research*, March 17, 2021, https://www.aier.org/article/more-covid-suicides-than-covid-deaths-in-kids/.

10 From analysis of 2019 Youth Risk Behavior Survey data.

There's no more important reality, directly and indirectly, in children's lives than their parents and immediate family. Yet they have no choice over this. Adult actions and decisions determine what kind of parents and families they have. To contradict the words of that classic song by the Who, "The kids are not alright." We adults are letting them down.

In contrast to these dismaying trends, we have biblical teaching about the value of children, and God's desire that, as much as possible, they be reared by loving, married parents. Increasingly, simply being committed to having children, doing so within healthy marriages, and raising them well are the most valuable, and counter-cultural, things that Christians can do.

In this chapter, I'll consider first what God says about children and the ideal connection of marriage to them. Then, I'll look briefly at the consequences of separating children from marriage. From there, I'll reflect on some of the practical challenges children bring into our marriages and remind us of solutions to these we've already considered. I also want to look at some of the challenges associated with procreation that so many couples face and briefly consider the issue of voluntary childlessness. Along the way, I hope to offer encouragement to those facing unwanted infertility, as well as single parents and stepparents.

GOD LOVES KIDS

At the beginning of the Bible, God creates humankind as male and female and immediately calls on them to procreate (Gen. 1:27–28). The first news we have of Adam and Eve following their expulsion from the garden is the conception and birth of Cain, for which Eve thanks the Lord (Gen. 4:1). The Psalms regularly present godly children as a blessing (cf. Ps. 127:3–5, 128:3b). After all, "children are a heritage from the Lord, the fruit of the womb a reward" (Ps. 127:3). As the Old Testament closes, Malachi told Hebrew men who were faithless to their marital covenants that one reason God was angry with them was because he was seeking "godly offspring" from their marital unions (2:15–16).

Moving into the New Testament, we see Jesus admonishing his disciples for turning away children, and infants being brought to him for blessing: "Let the little children come to me and do not hinder them, for to such belongs the kingdom of heaven" (Matt. 19:13–15; see also Luke 18:15–17). Then he laid his hands on the children and prayed for them. Christianity doesn't praise a world unhindered by children.

There's also nothing in the Bible to indicate that barrenness is something to be desired. Some good examples of barrenness are Abraham and Sarah (Gen. 16:1f), Samuel's mother Hannah (1 Sam. 1:5f), and Elizabeth, the mother of John the Baptist (Luke 1:24–25). Yes, God comforts and cares for the barren, and they're not cut off from a future in God's kingdom (Isa. 54:1–5). But that doesn't mean it's a state to be preferred.

We find that the Bible treats out-of-wedlock births similarly. It's not something to seek out or view neutrally (cf. Heb. 12:8). This is only logical since the Bible declares every sexual act outside of marriage to be sinful. Those in such circumstances, either as single parents or as children, are certainly not cut off from the Lord or in any way second-class citizens in his kingdom. We all come into saving faith through adoption and yet have all the privileges of being children of God (Gal. 4:4–7; Rom. 8:15–16). Nonetheless, having children within marriage is God's ideal.

Despite the fact that children are extolled as goods rather than hindrances no matter how they come to us, experiencing these blessings isn't automatic or without conditions. The Scriptures are full of examples and warnings of children bringing misery upon their parents and, often, the rest of society (cf. Deut. 21:18–21; Prov. 30:17). These outcomes are far more likely when, as the sad record of the priest Eli and his sons Hophni and Phineas illustrates (1 Sam. 2:12f), parents don't adequately instruct and discipline their children (see also Prov. 19:18, 23:13–14, 29:15; Heb. 12:10–11). This is why parents are admonished to diligently teach their children the ways of God (Deut. 4:9, 6:7, 11:19; Eph. 6:4).

Moreover, good parenting doesn't guarantee godly children. Indwelling sin is a powerful reality in all humankind. Our children aren't machines that always do what we want if we push the right buttons. Some of them reject godly instruction (cf. Prov. 12:1; 15:5). Children must ultimately choose to heed and to do what's right, which is why this is also commanded (Exod. 20:12; Prov. 1:7–9; Eph. 6:1). When we see wayward people, it's not necessarily true that they didn't have godly parents.

Still, we're called upon to take parenting seriously, to undertake it in accordance with God's moral laws, and to develop relationships with our children that don't make it unnecessarily hard for them to honor and obey us (cf. Eph. 6:4). Our model is Christ, and our aim is our children living righteously (cf. Heb. 12:9–10). We're to "bring them up in the discipline and instruction of the Lord" (Eph. 6:4b). Whatever we do is to be for the glory of God, even eating and drinking (1 Cor. 10:31). Doesn't that include parenting?

And it isn't just about our own efforts. Recognizing the sinfulness and inadequacy of all parents and children, we need to rely on the grace of God. We need to pray for ourselves and our children, seek godly guidance and instruction, and recognize that, while we carry the ultimate responsibility of parenting, our children need the instruction, friendship, input, and so on of many other people.

As a father of six, I've learned the hard way how important it is to simply love our children in word and in deed. After all, "love covers a multitude of sins (1 Pet. 4:8b). And I promise you, every parent sins against his or her children. When that happens, we must confess it to our children and ask their forgiveness. This not only brings reconciliation, but models godly humility and integrity for them.

There's a flipside to children being a gift of God. Yes, they are a gift, but they're from God. They ultimately belong to him, not us. We must give account to God for how we raise them, as they must someday give account to him for their own lives (Rom. 14:12). If God chooses to bless us with children, they're a trust, a responsibility, of which we're stewards.

Parenting is hard work and a grave responsibility. But ultimately, children supported, guided, and disciplined by godly parents will normally bring joy and blessing to their mother and father, their families, the church, and as good citizens, to society as a whole.

HAVING AND RAISING CHILDREN CAN BRING STRESS AND DISTRESS

When baby comes along, marital happiness often temporarily declines.[11] This is nothing compared to the negative impact of single parenting, but it's real nonetheless. Are we surprised? After all, "parents have to put up with the stresses of sleepless nights, toddler temper tantrums, and teenage sullenness, not to mention the time and money spent on their kids."[12] My wife and I dealt with this through six children and are now watching our married older daughters experiencing the same things.

---

11 Though claims of higher depression and risk of divorce for married, new parents are not accurate. See *When Baby Makes Three*, 13–15.

12 *When Baby Makes Three*, 14–15.

One important secret to coping with these challenges is simply to expect them. If we have a realistic rather than a pollyannish view of childrearing, we won't be as shocked and let down when the difficulties inevitably come.

It's also important to remember, in the midst of the strains, that children bring a lot of joy—all the more to the degree we value, cherish, love, and invest in them. Along with dirty diapers and sleepless nights are the baby's first steps; hearing "Mama" for the first time; watching them in their first ballet, dramatic performance, or sports event; and seeing them overcome adversity, find their callings, and become mature men and women.

Married parents with children are much more likely than married folk without them to say that their lives are characterized by "an important purpose."[13] They're responsible for someone outside themselves who needs them and who, God willing, will carry on after them.

When I looked into the eyes of each of my newborn infants, I saw a person made in the image of God who would live for eternity. This person had been placed into the hands of me and my wife—encircled by the support of our family, friends, and church—for a little while, but they belonged to God, bearing eternal souls. There's something awesome, in the true sense of that word, in having children. Don't miss that amidst the difficulties.

Finally, as *Baby Makes Three* abundantly documents, many of the most important keys to bearing the burdens and stress of having and successfully raising children with minimal negative impact upon our marital relationships are simply those associated with good marriage itself. We overviewed them in the last chapter: respect, kindness, generosity,

---

13 *When Baby Makes Three*, 16.

commitment, caring, forgiveness, sharing the load, good communication, investing quality time in our families, expecting conflict and handling it with grace and honesty, regularly participating in a local church, being embedded in supportive family and friendship networks, and even managing our money well. This also includes, when possible, resuming regular sexual relationships quickly following the inevitable disruptions that come with childbirth and infants.

There's a billboard I used to see a lot. It said something like this: "If you want to love your children, love their mother." That's profound. The foundation for sound parenting is a healthy marriage. Without that, as we've seen, parenting is just a lot harder. For those of us who are married and parents, we must never focus so much on parenting that we neglect the delights and duties of our marriages.

One more note here: If having children introduces stress even with the support of a loving spouse, how much more so for those who find themselves parenting alone or in other challenging circumstances? I want to encourage you that God will give you grace to persevere, and he provides the abundant support of your family, friends, and the local church. This ought to include not only spiritual encouragement but practical help. Those of us in the church should take seriously our calling to participate in the family of God, coming alongside single parent families in our congregations and serving as surrogate grandparents, uncles, aunts, and the like, helping to step into the space left by an absent parent.

PROCREATION CHALLENGES

The pain of married people who want to have children and can't is real. I've known many who have struggled with this. What can we say to them?

First, there's nothing about this that undermines the value and goodness of their marriages. This is ultimately part of God's sovereign plan, and it doesn't demean these individuals or their marriages. As some of the Scriptures I cited earlier attest with joy, there's no lack of purpose in God's kingdom, including as married persons, for those who haven't been able to experience pregnancy and childbirth.

Second, it's perfectly legitimate to explore ways—beyond adoption, which is a wonderful gift of God—to bear children. It's important to remember, though, that many of the options currently available to treat infertility are morally problematic. Side effects, including what happens if pregnancy with triplets or even more fetuses occurs, have to be honestly dealt with. All things considered, approaches that involve inseminating eggs outside the body, surrogates, donor eggs and sperm, and so on are the most ethically questionable. Couples shouldn't approach this without wise, biblical counsel and a clear understanding of what each option entails. The Bible is clear that we must never do something sinful even if we think good may come of it (Rom. 3:8). Hard as infertility is, this is true here too.[14]

One area that's relatively new and difficult is something called embryonic adoption, which is the implantation of frozen embryos stored by couples undergoing fertility treatment, which they don't intend to "use." I believe this is a form of legal adoption that's perfectly acceptable. The child is being rescued from a situation that the adoptive parents didn't create. In some ways, this is similar to the rescue of abandoned infants by early Christians in ancient Rome. Morally problematic medical interventions need not be involved.[15]

---

14 Ayers, *Christian Marriage*, 107–08.

15 Ayers, *Christian Marriage*, 108–09. There's an excellent discussion of this in Russell Moore's "Should Christians Adopt Embryos?", September 20, 2012, https://www.russellmoore.com/2012/09/20/should-christians-adopt-embryos/.

What about married Christians who voluntarily choose to remain childless? At the risk of being controversial, I find this hard to support biblically. This isn't about the appropriateness of using contraception to delay or limit childbearing. This isn't the same as choosing to marry if age, infertility, or other infirmity makes having children impossible or overly risky. This involves rejecting something that God clearly indicated is a central purpose of marriage.

Some will object to the stance I just stated. I've certainly had believing friends with whom I respectfully disagree on this. Yet I find no way around it. I'd encourage those intent on childless marriages to at least pray and seek God's counsel on this through Scripture, pastoral counsel, and reading arguments on both sides from those with a high view of the Bible. Given the abundant weight of biblical and historic Christian teaching on children and marriage, such a decision certainly shouldn't be taken lightly.

1. What do the Scriptures teach about the value of children? How and why do we so often fail to appreciate that?

2. In what ways, and why, has our culture increasingly come to view children more as a burden than a blessing?

3. What evidence do we have to support the Bible's claims that children should ideally be had and raised within the bonds of loving, committed marriages?

4. What encouragement can single parents, or those unable to have children, take from the word of God?

5. What difficulties should parents having children expect, and what are some ways they can manage and reduce those difficulties?

6. Why can we say that an important duty we owe our children is maintaining a healthy marriage?

7. What things should couples consider if they're unable to have children through natural procreation and choose to pursue fertility treatments?

8. If a couple is infertile, should they normally pursue having children either through adoption or fertility treatments?

9. What do you think about Christian married couples choosing to remain childless even if they're able to have children? What biblical support would you use to make your case?

So Why Would Anyone Get Married?

I like to characterize marriage as being like a geode. On the outside, it appears plain in many respects, beyond perhaps the wedding celebration and various celebratory moments. Two sinful people, committed to spend their lives together, having sexual relationships only with each other across often decades of time, typically raising children, growing old, enjoying good times, and enduring difficulties together. Two people who know that someday, in all likelihood in this fallen world, one will bury the other, and then live on, at least for a time.

Yet also like a geode, look inside and—at least in godly marriages—there's beauty, wonder, subtleties, and surprises. We see a mysterious revelation of the eternal bond between Christ and his people, a bond sealed with sacrifice and devotion. We see reflections of the Trinity, an infinite relationship marked by fruitful love. There's support and a bulwark against loneliness, the begetting of children made in the image of God who'll live forever, and we find holy sexual bonds that elevate husband and wife, celebrating and realizing the reality of two as one flesh. With our spiritual eyes we see that God created marriage when he made humankind and made marriage foundational to the world he meant for men and women to rule together.

Let me finish this booklet with a simple prayer:

Oh Lord God, King of the Universe, Creator of all things, we praise you for the institution of marriage. Your design for it is perfect and profoundly beautiful. You created it for your glory and our good. Yet we're a frail and sinful people handling high and holy responsibilities. Help us by your grace to understand your intentions and live by them faithfully, whether we're called to marriage or singleness, parenthood or living without children, through all of the difficulties and joys of life. May our marriages and families be a testament and blessing to the watching world. In Christ's precious name we pray.

WHY WOULD ANYONE GET MARRIED?

Made in the USA
Middletown, DE
12 July 2022

69047834R00040